THE LADY WITH THE SHIP ON HER HEAD

Harcourt Brace Jovanovich, Publishers
San Diego   New York   London

THE LADY
WITH THE SHIP
ON HER HEAD

Written and illustrated by
Deborah Nourse Lattimore

Copyright © 1990 by Deborah Nourse Lattimore

Requests for permission to make copies of any part of the work
should be mailed to: Copyrights and Permissions Department,
Harcourt Brace Jovanovich, Publishers, Orlando, Florida 32887.

Library of Congress Cataloging-in-Publication Data
Lattimore, Deborah Nourse.
The lady with the ship on her head.
Summary: Madame Pompenstance competes for the Best
Headdress Award at the annual Fancy Dress Ball, unaware
that a small ship has sailed onto her head and become
her headdress.
[1. Contests — Fiction.   2. Humorous stories]
I. Title.
PZ7.L36998Lad   1990   [E]   89-11218
ISBN 0-15-243525-5

First edition

A B C D E

The illustrations in this book were done in Winsor & Newton watercolors
on 90-lb. D'Arches hot-press paper.
The display type was set in Goudy Old Style by Thompson Type, San Diego, California,
and adapted by Eileen Boniecka / Persimmon Graphics.
The text type was set in Goudy Old Style by Thompson Type, San Diego, California.
Color separations were made by Bright Arts, Ltd., Hong Kong.
Printed and bound by Tien Wah Press, Singapore
Production supervision by Warren Wallerstein and Michele Weekes
Designed by Camilla Filancia

For my parents:

Marthermarie and Andrew, Richmond,

and Alice, who listened in the kitchen

For fifteen years Madame Pompenstance had wanted to win the Medal of Honor for the Best Headdress at the Fancy Dress Ball. But every year the Medal went to someone else, usually one of her friends. This year she planned many designs, but none seemed quite right. She hoped, as always, for a miracle.

When the day of the ball arrived, Madame Pompenstance strolled down to the beach. The seashore is a good place to clear one's mind, she thought.

The sand was littered with magnificent shells, beach flowers, shiny stones, and dried starfish. Perhaps a shell or two would do the trick, she said to herself, placing a few in her hair. It's not much, but it will be better than nothing.

Just at that moment a very small triple-masted sailing ship put into port. Madame Pompenstance bent over to admire a particularly handsome shell, and the small ship rowed right onto her head.

Strange, but the sun is beating down on my head in a rather fierce way, she thought.

Madame Pompenstance was invited that day to the villa of the Countess Eclair. When she arrived, all her friends were making their usual neat shots at a game of balls and hoops. But when Madame Pompenstance bent to take aim, the weight of the sailing ship threw her forward. She hit a strange curved ball that circled the hoops and knocked the other balls off the field.

"Who does she think she's fooling?" said Madame Moustarde. "We can all see that she's wearing her headdress for the ball tonight. And, I must say, that's the most ridiculous thing I've *ever* seen!"

"Maybe it gives her better balance," said Madame Romaine with a sniff. "She *is* winning the game."

Meanwhile, the swaying was noticed by the captain of the ship, who thought they were still at sea, and he yelled at his crew, "Drop those anchors!" This they did, and the anchors landed very neatly under Madame's earlobes. "OOOOOwww!" she cried and swung her mallet furiously. Her ball flew across the garden, hit Madame Moustarde's ball, and went through all the hoops. "Game!" cried the judge. "Game to Madame Pompenstance!"

This was the first time Madame Pompenstance had ever won at balls and hoops, but all she said was, "What a vise my head is in today."

Perhaps the High Tea Party is what I need, she said to herself and hurried away to the table. Everyone was chatting merrily except Madame Romaine, who bent close to Madame Moustarde and said, "That headdress has got to go!"

After the first cup of tea, Madame Pompenstance held her lorgnette to her eye and peered into her cup to read the tea leaves. Madame Romaine picked up a small smoked fish from one of the trays and wickedly tossed it at the jaunty little ship. The captain spotted the fish on deck, and in a flash the fish was spirited below.

That's funny, said Madame Romaine to herself. I know I just threw that fish,

but where did it go? So she threw a sticky bun onto the deck and then an orange slice. These, too, were hauled away by a happy crew.

The Countess noticed that the tea things were disappearing. "HmmHmm, Madame Romaine! It seems we are running out of tea things. Go ask the butler to bring more. And while you're away, Madame Pompenstance may pour for us." "Well, I never!" said Madame Romaine under her breath.

Despite the refreshment, the High Tea Party did not make Madame Pompenstance feel better. I've got to get my mind off that Fancy Dress Ball, she thought. All this thinking has given me a headache.

"Ah! A little entertainment!" she said—and joined the others who had just sat down to a game of cards.

But Madame Pompenstance couldn't concentrate at all. The headache wouldn't go away. Madame Poupé placed her cards down one by one with the utmost care, smiling devilishly. She thought she had the best hand, and all through the game she taunted Madame Pompenstance. "This is ridiculous!" snapped Madame Pompenstance, thinking only of her headache, and slammed her cards down on the table. It was a royal flush. "My dear!" exclaimed the Countess. "This is a first! Let us all congratulate Madame's success!"

But Madame Pompenstance, forehead in hand, gave her regrets and rushed away.

She hurried down the street for her last stop of the day at the portrait painter's salon. The afternoon wind blew up and the crew of the small ship hoisted the sails. This slowed Madame Pompenstance down and made her more snappish and crabby. By the time she reached the painter's salon, an angry blush had spread over her cheeks. "Madame looks perfectly splendid today!" said the painter.

"Madame feels perfectly dreadful!" She glared at him and tried to sit still.

Meanwhile, out on the street, Mesdames Moustarde, Romaine, Poupé, and LePeaux passed by and cried, "Look at that! What conceit! Having her portrait painted with that ship on her head! I suppose she thinks she's going to win tonight." And they all rushed home to get ready.

Time drew near for the Fancy Dress Ball. Madame Pompenstance returned from the salon and sat in her dressing room, swaying this way and that. Her ladies-in-waiting fussed and fiddled and flattered her.

"Madame will surely win the Medal for the Best Headdress this year, no?"

But Madame was in no mood to be humored.

Another Fancy Dress Ball and no Medal! she thought bitterly. I haven't been able to come up with a single idea all day, so those silly shells will just have to do.

Madame Pompenstance was among the last to arrive at the King's palace. She stood up tall, despite her throbbing head, and stepped carefully down the Grand Staircase. She was a splendid sight!

When at last the time came for the judging of the Best Headdress, the ladies assembled. Madame LePeaux followed Madame Pompenstance down the Grand Staircase and spilled her glass of rum punch onto the deck of the small ship. That should fix her! she said to herself. The crew ran to their buckets and mops and began to scrub the deck. They soon discovered that it was not sea-water but rum punch. They filled their buckets and scurried into the cabin to have a party.

Meanwhile, Madame Pompenstance waited for the judges, among whom was the King himself. She glanced down the line at the competition. Madame Moustarde's hairdo was musical, with a small gold lyre and sheets of music arranged on her head. Madame Romaine's wig had little gold cupids with arrows and candy hearts, a tribute to love. Madame Poupé's headdress was an elaborate fountain that splashed over the front of her dress. Everyone tried not to notice how wet she was getting. But Madame LePeaux's wig was the most original. It had a large gold birdcage with a real canary inside twittering and chirruping. And I've got only shells—I'll lose again, Madame Pompenstance thought miserably.

The judges approached. By this time the ship's pitching, as the excited crew hauled buckets of rum to the cabin and ran back to the deck again, was making Madame dizzy. She braced herself and tried to stand up straight. Just as the King stopped in front of Madame Pompenstance, the cabin lights went on in the small ship. "Remarkable!" he exclaimed. "A tribute to seafaring! And so cleverly arranged! Notice the earrings! Why, even the stiff way she's standing reminds one of a ship's figurehead!" The judges circled the King and conferred. In thirty seconds they announced their decision: "The winner of the Medal for Best Headdress is Madame Pompenstance!" Everyone applauded wildly—everyone except Madame Moustarde, Madame Romaine, Madame Poupé, and Madame LePeaux, who stamped her foot angrily while the canary flapped around the cage screeching.

But Madame Pompenstance heard no screeching or cheering. Her head had gotten the better of her. The crew was now dancing on the deck and singing sea chanteys. Madame Pompenstance dashed from the room, her head in her hands.

She ran down the street yelling, "What shall I do? What *shall* I do?" She stopped near the path to the ocean. "Aah! An ocean breeze!" She raced to the beach, tripped over a rock, and fell facedown in the sand at the water's edge. The anchors popped off her ears and the very small triple-masted sailing ship set out to sea.

All of a sudden Madame Pompenstance felt better. She shook the sand from her face. The shells she had put in her hair that morning fell into the sand in front of her. "So that's it!" she cried. "No *wonder* I had a headache! Award or no award, I'll never wear shells again!"

And she stood up and made her way carefully home.